BOLDPRINT

True Crime

JACK BOOTH • BOB KNUCKLE

Editorial Board

David Booth • Joan Green • Jack Booth

CRIME SCENE DO NOT CROSS

STECK-VAUGHN
Harcourt Achieve

www.HarcourtAchieve.com

10801 N. Mopac Expressway
Building # 3
Austin, TX 78759
1.800.531.5015

Steck-Vaughn is a trademark of Harcourt Achieve Inc. registered in the United States of America and/or other jurisdictions. All inquiries should be mailed to Harcourt Achieve Inc., P.O. Box 27010, Austin, TX 78755.

Rubicon © 2006 Rubicon Publishing Inc.
www.rubiconpublishing.com

All rights reserved. No part of this publication may be reproduced or transmitted in any form or by any means, electronic or mechanical, including photocopying, recording, taping, or any information storage and retrieval system, without permission in writing from the copyright owner.

Project Editors: Miriam Bardswich, Kim Koh
Editorial Assistant: Erin Doupe
Art/Creative Director: Jennifer Drew-Tremblay
Designer: Jeanette Debusschere

6 7 8 9 10   5 4 3 2 1

True Crime
ISBN 1-41902-458-2

CONTENTS

4 Introduction: Crime Scene Investigator
Think you've got what it takes to be a Crime Scene Investigator? Put your skills to the test in this CSI Challenge.

6 Greatest Heists
From cash to racehorses, descriptions of daring heists in history.

9 The Flying Bandit
Gilbert "The Flying Bandit" Galvan was a one-man crime wave. This true account tells of his incredible string of robberies.

12 In the Line of Duty
His madness lasted only minutes, but Adrian Humers left a trail of pain and death in this tragic true account.

16 18 Methods of Execution
Ouch! If you do the crime, you've got to pay the price — 18 gripping descriptions that will make you cringe and say "Owwww."

20 The Cask of Amontillado
A chilling thriller comes to life in this vibrant graphic story.

24 The Poisoner
Murder in Canada! Murder in India! Follow the trail (if you can) in this true account of two detectives chasing a murderer around the world.

27 Reflections of a Police Officer
Inspector Warren Korol gives us a review of the lessons he learned chasing down "The Poisoner."

28 Infamous Prisons
Descriptions of some of the darkest prisons in the world.

33 I'm Outta Here!
True accounts of incredible prison escapes.

34 Ma Barker: The FBI's Most Wanted Woman
Read this true account of the mother and son team that J. Edgar Hoover once called "the toughest gang of hoodlums."

36 Lizzie Borden: Did She or Didn't She?
Lizzie Borden — quiet Sunday school teacher or homicidal maniac? Read this true account.

38 Double Take
A twisted tale of crime fiction.

44 The Woman Who Stalks the Stalkers
An interview with a modern-age crime fighter: profiler Dr. Miki Pistorius.

46 CSI: Crime Scene Investigation
How real are the heroics of the popular television CSI Units? Find out in this eye-opening explanation.

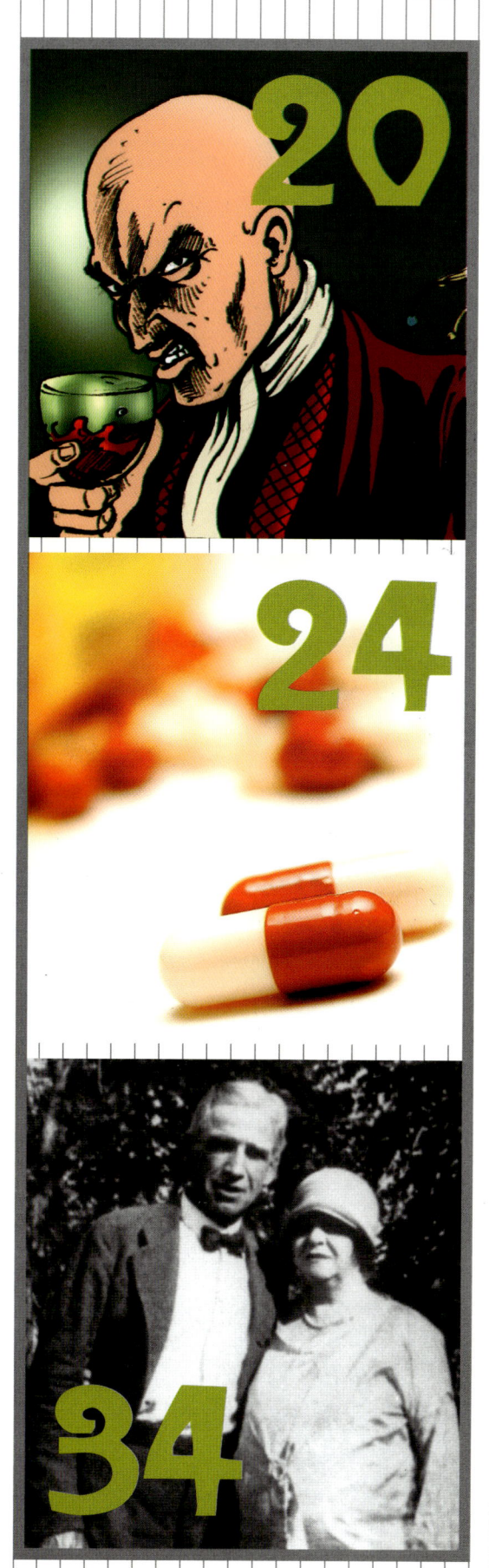

CRIME SCENE INVESTIGATOR
First Day on the Job

Just imagine. You've got your university degree in forensic science. You've been hired as a crime scene investigator. This is your first day on the job. You've got a murder scene to investigate.

What thoughts might you have as you travel to the crime scene?

You're at the crime scene. It's a local man's home. As you carefully enter through the front door, you see the body on the living-room floor. It looks like there's a knife wound in his chest. However, you don't see a knife. But you do see two weapons near the body. There is a gun on the floor next to the victim's bloody hand. It's an antique dueling pistol. There's another gun — a revolver — on the coffee table beside the victim.

On the other side of the room, you notice a small pool of blood on the carpet close to the wall. You carefully cross the room to examine the blood. You notice an obvious indentation in the carpet — a sign that someone or something had been lying there. You see two black fibers inside the indentation. When you look up, you see four bullets stuck in the wall.

As you are photographing the bullets in the wall, a police officer informs you that the window above the kitchen sink has been smashed. There are three bloody fingerprints on the kitchen counter. You go to the kitchen and notice a footprint on the tile floor in front of the sink.

It looks like the killer entered the victim's house through the kitchen window. Looking over the crime scene again, you know what you have to do. There are questions to be answered.

All images–istockphoto

CSI TOOLS:

MIKROSIL
A thick putty used to develop casts of wounds. It's like the material dentists use to make molds of teeth.

CODIS
Combined DNA Index System: A computer program that compares the Convicted Offender Directory, which contains DNA records of criminals, to the Forensic Index, which documents DNA collected at crime scenes. CODIS helps police and crime scene investigators in identifying serial criminals.

MICROSPECTROPHOTOMETER
A device used to examine the color of fibers. A precise color match indicates a fiber match.

AFIS
Automated Fingerprint Identification System: A computer network that scans fingerprints found at crime scenes and compares them with fingerprints collected by police and crime scene investigators around the world. The print is traced and scanned into the computer by a fingerprint expert.

SLIP
Shoewear Linking and Identification Program: A computer program that contains pictures of shoes no longer manufactured by shoe companies. The program allows police and crime scene investigators to identify shoe prints left at crime scenes.

COMPARISON MICROSCOPE
A double microscope that allows two different objects to be viewed at the same time. Firearm comparisons, for example, are done using the comparison microscope.

FINGERPRINT BRUSH
A brush used to apply powder to a surface that may have fingerprints. This brush is made from fiberglass, camel hair, or squirrel hair.

RUBBER-GELATIN LIFTERS
Gel used to lift finger, foot, and shoe prints from flat surfaces such as flooring, wood, and paper. These prints are not always visible to the human eye.

CSI CHALLENGE

Which CSI tools would you use to help answer each of these questions?

1. What type of knife was used to kill the victim?

2. Who fired the four bullets into the wall?

3. Which gun did the bullets come from?

4. If the blood located in the indentation in the carpet is the killer's, is the killer a serial killer?

5. What type of material did the two black fibers come from? Are there more fibers?

6. How will the bloody fingerprints from the wooden kitchen counter be removed? To whom do the fingerprints belong?

7. What type of shoe made the footprint on the kitchen floor?

Check this out! You've been trained. You've got these tools. You know how to use them.

As you read through this book consider these tools. You are the crime scene investigator.

GREATEST HEISTS

> ### warm up
> What is a heist? How is it different from a robbery, burglary, or theft?

The Brinks Job

Brinks Inc. is a company that takes care of large sums of money for banks and other institutions. In January 1950, robbers successfully raided the "burglar-proof" Boston headquarters of Brinks Inc.

They walked out of the Brinks office with $2.7 million. However, they were not exactly master criminals. While waiting for things to cool down before sharing the money, two of the gang members stole a lawnmower. Police officers looking for the lost lawnmower found it — in the same car trunk where the gang's guns were hidden. Guns, fingerprints, more searches, jail time …

Police question Brinks' employees in the vault room on the night of the robbery. The open vault is in the background.

The Great Train Robbery

On August 8, 1963, 15 masked men stopped the Glasgow to London train by resetting the train signals beside the tracks.

The robbers swarmed the train, badly injuring the driver during the attack. They grabbed 120 bags containing £2.6 million in used bills.

Police quickly found the hideout of "The Great Train Robbers." There, in the farmhouse, police found fingerprints. One thing always leads to another.

Members of the gang were tried and given sentences totalling 300 years. Most of the money was never found.

Ronnie Biggs, the leader, escaped from prison in 1965. He returned to England from Brazil in 2001. He wanted to spend the last years of his life at home in England. He will. He has to serve the remainder of his 30-year sentence.

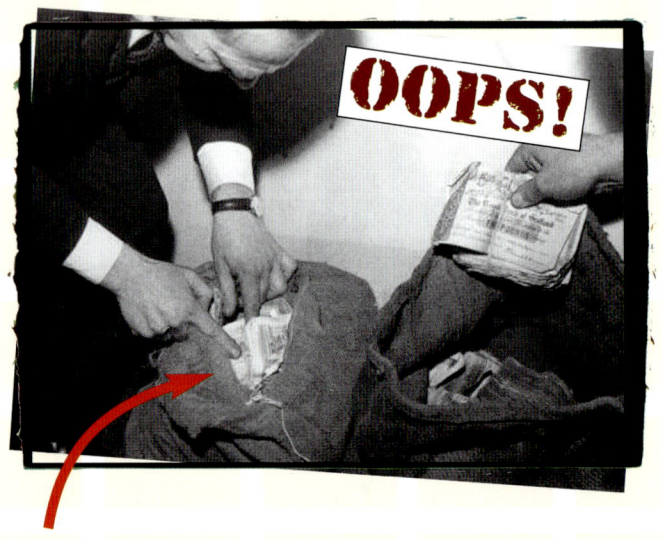

Train robbery cash? Scotland Yard detectives inspect two sacks of banknotes, believed to be part of the proceeds of the Great Train Robbery, after they were found in a telephone booth in London. The loot was discovered after an anonymous telephone call to the police.

Shergar

In 1983, Shergar, one of the best racehorses of all time, was stolen. Sean O'Callaghan, a convicted murderer who became an informer against the IRA, says in his book, *The Informer* (1998), that Shergar died because the IRA horsenappers couldn't handle it.

"To handle Shergar, the IRA recruited a man who had once 'worked with horses.' But working with horses is one thing: dealing with a thoroughbred stallion, which can be a difficult, highly-strung creature at the best of times, is another story altogether."

The horse got out of control, and injured itself. Unable to handle him, the gang killed Shergar just days after stealing him. The thieves still tried to get a $10 million ransom from the owner, the Aga Khan, an Indian prince. He wouldn't pay without seeing the horse. No horse — no ransom.

Whatever happened to Shergar?

Boston Art Theft

In March 1990, two men wearing fake moustaches and police uniforms bluffed their way into the Isabella Stewart Gardner Museum in Boston, Massachusetts. They left with a dozen paintings by Rembrandt, Manet, Degas, and Vermeer — all famous and valued at the time at $300 million.

Some people think that IRA terrorists were behind the raid, hoping to negotiate a ransom for the paintings. But no one knows for sure. The paintings have not been seen since the robbery. The museum has offered a $5 million reward for information leading to their return. Any takers?

The Biggest Successful Jewelry Robbery

The *Guinness Book of Records* says the world's biggest jewelry robbery took place in August 1994, when three thieves burst into the Carlton Hotel in Cannes, France.

Firing machine guns, the thieves robbed the Carlton's jewelry store just as it was closing. They made off with $50 million worth of jewels. Later, the police discovered that the bullets the thieves had been firing were blanks. What happened to the loot? Nobody knows? Nobody?

They stole $50 million worth of jewels and never got caught. It seemed like the perfect crime.

IRA: Irish Republican Army, an Irish Catholic terrorist organization seeking the unity of Northern Ireland with the Irish Republic

Oslo Art Theft

It took four Norwegians less than a minute to steal Edvard Munch's painting, *The Scream,* from the Oslo National Museum in 1994. Two of the thieves climbed a ladder and got in through one of the art gallery's windows.

They planned to sell the painting, valued at $50 million, to the highest bidder.

Scotland Yard detectives pretended to be buyers interested in the stolen painting. They offered $600,000 to buy it — no questions asked. A meeting was arranged. The Norwegian police happened to be at the meeting. Guess what happened?

BUSTED

At the Scotland Yard sting operation, the thieves are caught in the act and arrested.

An Inside Job: Heathrow Airport

In February 2002, robbers got away with more than $6 million in cash in a raid on a British Airways security van at Heathrow Airport.

The theft happened in a secure area where ordinary passengers and workers were not allowed to go. The police thought the robbers must have had legitimate security passes.

The thieves escaped in a vehicle with British Airways markings. It was later found abandoned and burned.

Four people are now serving 25 years in prison. One of them was a security guard.

The police suspected the security guard and a few of his friends and relatives. They videotaped several conversations the gang had. The police hired a lip-reader to tell them what the gang was saying. Busted!

DOH!

Video surveillance and a lip-reader: a convicting combination.

The World's Most Famous Smile: Who Took the Mona Lisa?

On Monday, August 21, 1911, Leonardo da Vinci's *Mona Lisa* was stolen from the Louvre museum in Paris by an Italian named Vincenzo Perugia. He said he stole the painting out of patriotism. He didn't think that such a famous painting by an Italian should be in France.

Perugia spent Sunday night in the Louvre, hiding in a little room. While the museum was closed, he took the painting and cut it from its frame. Then, he just walked out of the museum. Don't try that today!

The painting was recovered 27 months later.

---

wrap up

1. Heist movies are popular. Which one of these heists do you think would work well as a movie? Would it be a comedy, a documentary, a thriller, …?

2. Design a poster to advertise your movie. Remember: title, stars, attention-grabbing description, etc.

The Flying Bandit

Gilbert Galvan was raised in a poor, troubled home in Los Angeles. His father was an abusive drunk. His mother was an unreliable, unpredictable woman who often abandoned Gilbert, his two brothers, and four sisters.

As Gilbert grew bigger and stronger, he became difficult to control and was constantly in trouble with the law for stealing and other acts of juvenile delinquency. After his parents spilt up permanently, his mother could not handle him and he was sent to a military school in Texas. The authorities there couldn't cope with him either and expelled him at the age of 14. He spent the next three years in a foster home, then went out on his own, living a life that switched between part-time jobs and petty crime.

At 19, Gilbert committed his first major felony, stealing a safe from a store. By the time he was in his twenties, he began a one-man crime wave, committing armed robberies in Illinois, Idaho, Wisconsin, and Colorado. Caught and convicted, he was sentenced to eight years in the Federal Correctional Institute at Oxford, Wisconsin. It was here that prison officials described Gilbert as being intelligent, charming, and friendly. They also identified him as a sociopath, a person without morals who shows little concern for the welfare of others. His Oxford parole officer believed that Gilbert thrived on the thrill of committing

---

felony: *a serious crime, usually violent*

warm up

- In some places, a career criminal can be put in prison for an undetermined length of time — maybe forever.

- What do you think would make a judge decide if someone is a career criminal?

CHECKPOINT

Watch out for this guy! He's intelligent, charming, and friendly. He's also a sociopath. As you continue reading, watch for signs of both sides of his personality.

WANTED

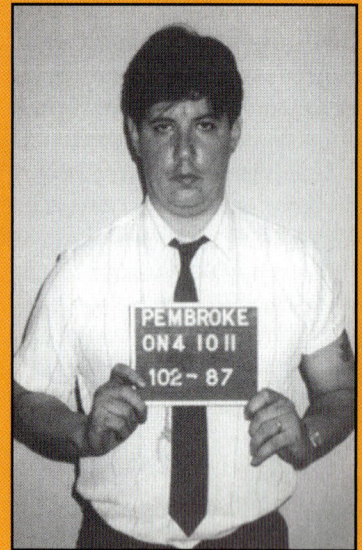

Gilbert Galvan was dubbed "The Flying Bandit." Galvan robbed 59 banks and jewelry stores from Vancouver to Halifax from 1984-1987.

> **CHECKPOINT**
> What makes this guy a magnet for women? How does he fool them?

crimes. She claimed he loved the challenge of planning a crime and took great pleasure in carrying it out and not getting caught.

After Gilbert was paroled in September 1982, he scurried around the country committing burglaries until he was arrested red-handed, trying to swindle a Western Union Office out of $4.5 million in Three Rivers, Michigan, a small town 140 miles west of Detroit.

When the police checked Gilbert's car, they found a number of birth certificates he was using as aliases. They also determined he was a parolee wanted by police in three states.

Held without bail in a small county jail, Gilbert knew he had to escape from it before he was transferred to a state pen where the security would be much more strict. He found his opportunity one night using a pool cue, with a paper clip attached to it, to steal some prison keys through the bars of the guard's office.

Once he was free, he phoned a female friend to help him. Because his trail was too hot to remain in the United States, he had the woman drive to Detroit. Then they crossed the border into Canada.

After they spent a night in a motel, Gilbert borrowed money from her. Against her wishes he deserted her and hitchhiked to Toronto. Then he took a cheap room in a men's hostel and managed to buy a birth certificate and a social insurance card from a down-and-out-drunk named Robert Whiteman. From that day forward, Gilbert assumed this new identity.

From Toronto, Robert Whiteman hitchhiked to Ottawa, got a room in another hostel, and soon found work as a "Frostee" bicycle ice cream salesman. He met Janice, a social worker, at the hostel. Robert had always been a magnet for women and before long he and Janice were dating. They married, and soon she was expecting a baby. To support his family, Robert told his wife that he was working for his father on a job that required him to install security systems all across Canada. In truth, Robert was flying to cities from coast to coast robbing banks and jewelry stores.

---

hostel: *temporary shelter*

During his off-hours in Ottawa, Gilbert began hanging around a sleazy strip club and became close friends with some of Ottawa's criminals. This caused a lot of tension between Robert and his wife. To appease her, Gilbert agreed to move away from his wicked friends and settle his family in nearby rural Pembroke.

But that didn't stop his thievery. He continued flying and over a period of 33 months committed 59 robberies, sometimes two in one day, for a total take of almost $2 million.

During this time, Robert developed a cocaine addiction that used up much of his stolen loot. Eventually, one of his criminal associates, who was trying to save himself from a stiff prison sentence, ratted Robert out to the police.

They immediately put Robert under surveillance, and within weeks, arrested him at the Pembroke airport as he returned from a bank robbery with thousands of dollars of stolen cash on his person.

Dubbed "The Flying Bandit" by the press, in 1988 Gilbert confessed to all his crimes and was sentenced to 20 years in a Canadian penitentiary. In 1996 he was released to the U.S. on a prisoner exchange program and began serving "time owing" in three different states.

Gilbert was paroled from Oxford, Wisconsin in 1998 and opened his own commercial painting company. As his business flourished, he even took over the care of his older daughter who had become somewhat difficult for Gilbert's estranged wife to handle. Then sadly, Gilbert went back to his old ways and was captured robbing a town bank in McHenry, Illinois.

Gilbert could have received a life sentence for his many repeat offenses. Mercifully the judge acknowledged that in all of his robberies Gilbert had never harmed anyone. He sentenced Gilbert to eight years back at Oxford where he will remain until he is 52 years of age.

The sentence was just and necessary. Nevertheless, it does seem a shame that such a bright, likable, and talented man has wasted so much potential.

appease: *calm down*
surveillance: *close observation*

Some Thoughts From The Flying Bandit

In all honesty, it was never a conscious choice to make crime a living. From approximately the age of eight years old I was basically a state-raised kid. Some of the places I was sent to were kind of tough and I don't mean you were beat or abused but you were sent to these places and they were to feed you, clothe you, and give you a dry, safe place to sleep — a no frills way of raising a kid. Basically you were on your own for all the rest of whatever it is a kid wants growing up and you learned how to get those things from the only real life teachers available, the older kids — good kids — bad kids, etc. etc. I seemed to be attracted to the thieves but I also did not want to harm people. I knew from a very young age that 1) I liked being with people and 2) I was a thief. The latter just seemed to come second nature …

— Letter from Gilbert Galvan

wrap up

1. Think of three or four words you would use to describe Gilbert Galvan. Try not to use the descriptive words from the article. After each of your words, explain why you think the word is appropriate.

2. The author of this article has also written a book about The Flying Bandit. Imagine that you want to convince a Hollywood producer to make a movie about The Flying Bandit. Write a short letter explaining why it would make a good movie.

IN THE LINE OF DUTY

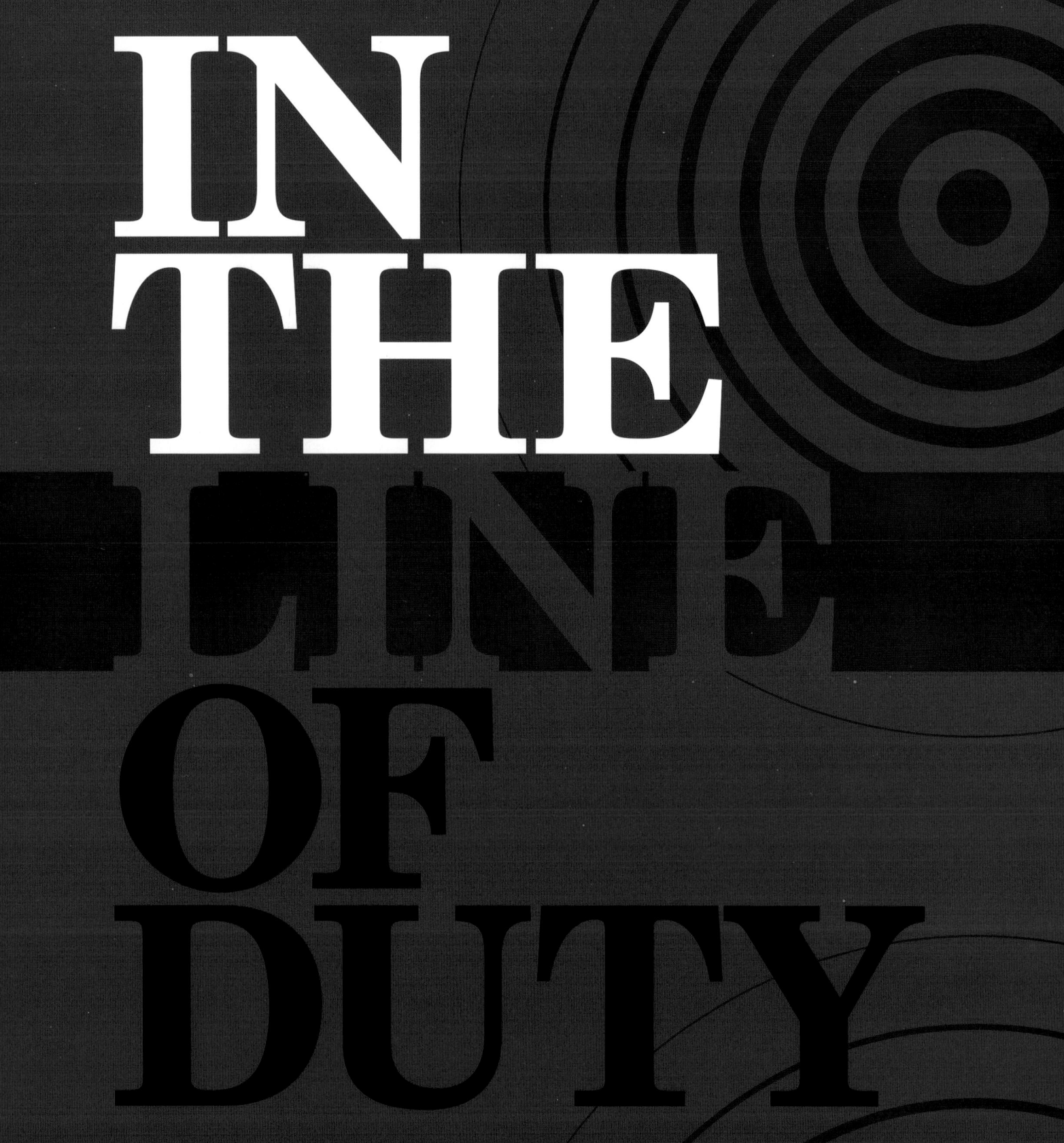

When Humes aimed Wally's stolen police pistol at them, the three Riverdale policemen responded with deadly force.

Detective William "Wally" Rolniak, a U.S. Air Force veteran was in his fourteenth year of service with the Riverdale Police Department. Riverdale, Illinois is a suburb of Chicago — a community of 16,500 that is served by a police force of 35 officers.

On the evening of February 4, 2004, Detective Rolniak was at the end of his shift when he was asked to escort a prisoner, Adrian Humes, from an interview room to the Riverdale cells.

Humes, 27, had used a firearm earlier that day to kidnap his ex-girlfriend from her parents' home. Only a few hours after this incident, he was arrested by a four-man Chicago police tactical team as he and the abducted woman were boarding a bus at the Chicago Greyhound Bus Terminal. He was brought to the Riverdale station for questioning.

The criminal system in Illinois states that anyone charged with a felony must be interviewed by representatives of the state. They will determine whether or not the case should go to trial.

Around 8:00 PM, Humes had just finished his lengthy interview with two assistant state's attorneys. It was their decision that he should be charged with counts of home

---

felony: *usually a violent crime, punishable by more than one year in prison*

warm up

- People choose different jobs or professions for a variety of reasons. Have an informal group or class discussion about what jobs you would like to have later in your lives. Who/what influences your job choices?

- Talk about what makes a young man or woman decide to become a police officer.

invasion, aggravated kidnapping, and attempted murder. Humes was to be booked and held in the Riverdale cells prior to his court appearance the following day.

Wally Rolniak, 39, was a highly respected lawman who had an extremely nice way of dealing with everyone including people who were charged with serious crimes.

Wally was assigned to take Humes down for fingerprinting. Although Humes was 6'4" and 260 pounds, he seemed quiet and cooperative. Wally decided not to put him in handcuffs for the short walk to booking and fingerprinting.

> **CHECKPOINT**
> What bad decision did Wally make here? Why do you think he did that?

When Wally's partner, Detective Sergeant Dan Dempsey, asked Wally if he needed any assistance. Wally declined.

"You finish your paperwork, Dan," Wally said, "I'll take him down by myself."

So Wally, dressed casually in plainclothes and wearing his favorite baseball cap, led Adrian Humes quietly away to be fingerprinted.

Moments later, Dan Dempsey heard loud voices coming from the stairs below and went to investigate. When he got there, he spotted Wally's baseball hat lying on the floor and heard the click of the nearby fire door as it was closing. By law, this is the only door in the police station that doesn't require a secret code to open.

> **CHECKPOINT**
> Think about it. Why should a fire door not require a secret code to open?

Suspecting that something was wrong, Dan opened the fire door and looked outside. There, about thirty yards away, was his partner Wally moving along the sidewalk with his hands up. And behind him was Adrian Humes holding a gun to Wally's head. Humes had physically turned on Wally in the police station and wrestled the gun from his holster. Now Wally's life was in danger.

Dempsey radioed the situation to the Riverdale police dispatcher. He also kept following Humes at a distance of 100 yards as Humes forced his captive to cross 138th Street and move past the Par Four Tavern. Wally looked back and made eye contact with Dan Dempsey.

"There was a look of relief in his eyes," Dempsey says. "He knew we were coming to help him."

Suddenly Adrian Humes turned and opened fire on Dan Dempsey. Right after that, Humes and Wally disappeared around the corner of the building.

As Dempsey cautiously edged his way to that corner, he heard more shots. He ran to the corner, carefully peered around it, and was shocked to see Wally lying on the ground. He wasn't moving.

More police arrived on the scene. 138th Street was blocked off in both directions. The search was on for Adrian Humes. Some suspected that he might have made a run for the wooded area behind the tavern. Several of the uniformed officers headed in that direction.

But Humes hadn't run for the woods. He had boldly gone out on 138th Street and had tried to carjack three different vehicles. The first driver ignored his gun threats and sped off. The second was a 71-year-old man who refused to let Humes get in his car. Humes shot him in the leg but the older man managed to drive away. He drove home and reported the incident to the police. The third was the driver of a pickup truck who bravely resisted Humes.

As Humes threatened him with death, the truck driver grabbed for Humes' gun and tried to wrestle it away.

By then, Dan Dempsey, and his brother Sgt. John Dempsey, and patrolman David Sinde were approaching the pickup truck with their guns drawn.

When Humes aimed Wally's stolen police pistol at them, the three Riverdale policemen responded with deadly force. Within a matter of seconds, they hit Humes with four shots to the chest. He died in the cab of the pickup truck.

Wally Rolniak had been taken to Christ Medical Center, but he was pronounced dead on arrival. He had been killed with two shots to the head.

Detective William "Wally" Rolniak is mourned and sadly missed by his widow Maureen and their two teen-aged daughters. He will be remembered by his many friends and colleagues. He is honored here as another American hero who sacrificed his life "In the Line of Duty."

CHECKPOINT
Why do police suggest that you don't resist in situations like this? They say to give the person with the gun what he/she wants.

Detective William "Wally" Rolniak

wrap up

1. Some people think that a person who kills a police officer should get a worse punishment than someone who kills a civilian. What do you think? Survey your group or class. How many people feel each way? List possible reasons for both points of view.

2. Imagine you are going to make a one-hour documentary film of "In the Line of Duty." You are going to use actors and real locations. Work with a partner to storyboard your film.

18 Methods of

⚠ WARNING This article contains subject matter that may offend some readers.

Ancient

1 STONING

The victims were killed by having stones thrown at them. This method was used for prostitutes, adulterers, and murderers.

2 CRUSHING BY ELEPHANT

For over 4,000 years crushing by elephant was a common sentence for those condemned to death throughout South and Southeast Asia. Sometimes the elephants ran their teeth through the body and tore it into pieces. The Romans and Carthaginians also used this method on occasion.

3 DEATH BY 1,000 CUTS

A small portion of flesh was cut from the victim's body every day until death resulted. This method was used in ancient China.

4 CRUCIFIXION

This refers to nailing or tying a victim to a cross until death. It was practiced in ancient times in the Middle East and used by the Romans against political enemies, especially slaves and Jews.

Medieval

5 SAWING

The condemned was hung upside down and then sawn apart down the middle. This method was used in the Spanish Inquisition (1478-1834) as a punishment for heresy (beliefs against a certain religion).

6 TEARING APART BY HORSES

The victim had his arms tied to one horse and his legs tied to another horse. The horses were driven on the run in opposite directions tearing the victim apart at the waist. This method was used in Russia in the 18th century.

EXECUTION

7 BEHEADING

This was done by sword, ax, or gibbet (a mechanical device). It is most often associated with medieval Germany and England. The last beheading took place in England in 1747.

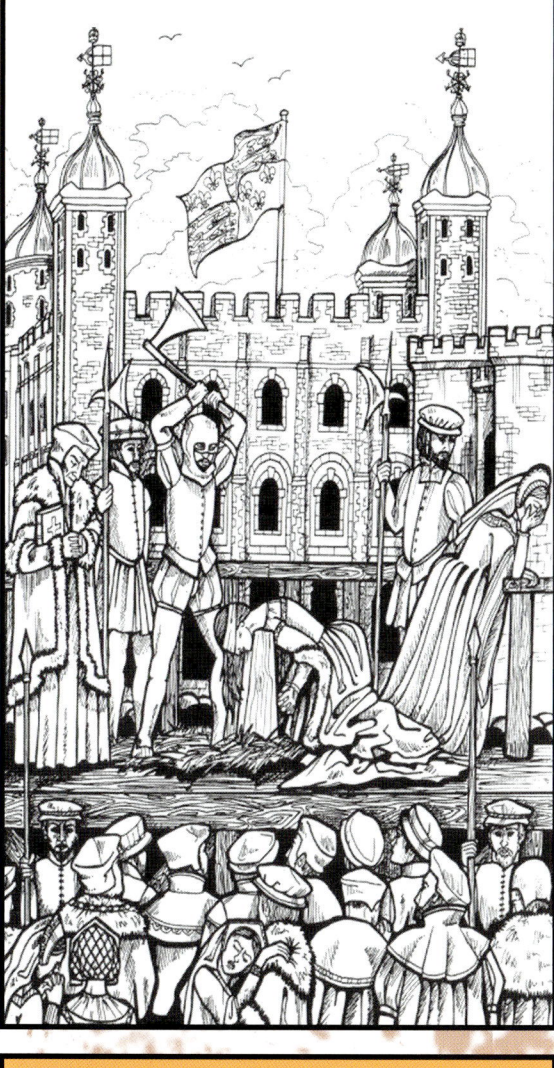

8 DRAWING AND QUARTERING

From 1283 to 1867, this was the punishment used in England for treason. First the victim was "drawn" on a hurdle (a sledge) to the place of execution. Then he was hanged, cut down before he died, and his internal organs were removed and burned before his eyes. He was beheaded and his body cut into quarters. His severed head was put on display for all to see.

9 THE WHEEL

The victim was tied to the outside of a wagon wheel and rolled over rough and jagged surfaces until death. Or, the wheel was laid on its side and the victim was stretched out and tied to the wheel. People beat the victim as the wheel was dragged through the streets.

10 IMPALEMENT

A sharpened stake was driven either from side to side or lengthwise through the victim's body. The stake was then driven into the ground so that others could witness the agony of the condemned. It was used extensively by Vladimir III (Vlad the Impaler) in Transylvania, Ivan the Terrible in Russia, and Nero in Rome.

11 BURNING AT THE STAKE

The victim was tied to a large stake and surrounded by brush and wood which was then set on fire. This method was used for crimes such as heresy, treason, and witchcraft.

Modern

12 GAS CHAMBER

First used in 1924 in Nevada, and most often in California. This method has been replaced with lethal injection in most jurisdictions. The victim is enclosed in an airtight chamber and killed with hydrogen cyanide gas.

13 THE GUILLOTINE

This is a machine for beheading victims invented by Dr. Joseph Guillotin. He wanted to make a victim's death less painful than some of the cruel methods used in earlier years. Widely used during the French Revolution (1789), the guillotine was last employed by France to execute a murderer in 1977.

14 THE GARROTE

This is a system of strangulation where an iron collar is slowly tightened around the victim's neck. As the collar tightened, a metal screw was also being driven into the back of the victim's neck to sever the spinal cord. From 1813 to 1974, this was the method of execution in Spain. Capital punishment was ended there in 1978.

15 HANGING

Hanging dates back to the 5th century. Early methods involved placing a rope around the neck of the convict, slowly drawing up and strangling the person. Sometimes the convicted person was forced to climb a ladder or stand in a cart which was then taken away. Later, gallows were built. The victim climbed up to a platform; a noose was placed around the neck and the trap door opened. The fall was supposed to snap the neck or cause strangulation.

16 LETHAL INJECTION

First used in Oklahoma in 1977. The victim is injected with chemicals that cause death. This method is used in 36 of the 38 states in the US that have the death penalty.

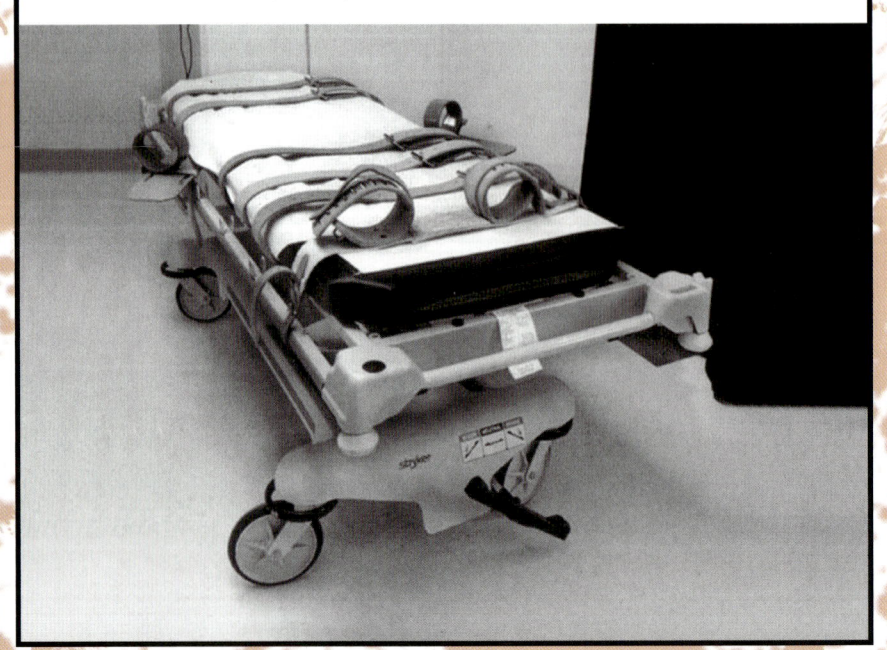

17 FIRING SQUAD

The victim is bound, seated on a chair or tied to a post, and shot with rifles by a squad of five men or more. This method is often associated with military executions. The last American states to employ this method were Utah and Idaho.

18 ELECTROCUTION

A jolt of electricity between 500 and 2,000 volts is passed through a victim's body for about 30 seconds. First used in New York State in 1888, it is now rarely used throughout the US.

wrap up

1. All of these methods of execution were used by governments supporting capital punishment. What is the status of capital punishment where you live? Now? In the past?

2. As you can see, many governments or legal systems moved, over time, from one method of execution to another. Why do you think they would stop one method of execution and switch to another?

3. You want to be proud of the society you live in. Is there room in a civilized society for capital punishment? Set up a debate or discussion in your class, making sure that you have both points of view.

FYI

- Capital Punishment: *capital* comes from the Latin *caput* meaning head.

- Hamida Djandoubi was the last person to be guillotined on September 10, 1977, at Baumettes Prison in Marseilles. He was an immigrant from Tunisia and had been convicted of murder.

- Although it was common in South Asia for rulers to use elephants as executioners, the Mogul Emperor Akbar (1547-1605) used his favorite elephant as a judge as well as an executioner. He believed that his favorite royal elephant could tell by instinct who was guilty of an offense or who was innocent.

THE CASK OF AMONTILLADO

Adapted from EDGAR ALLAN POE

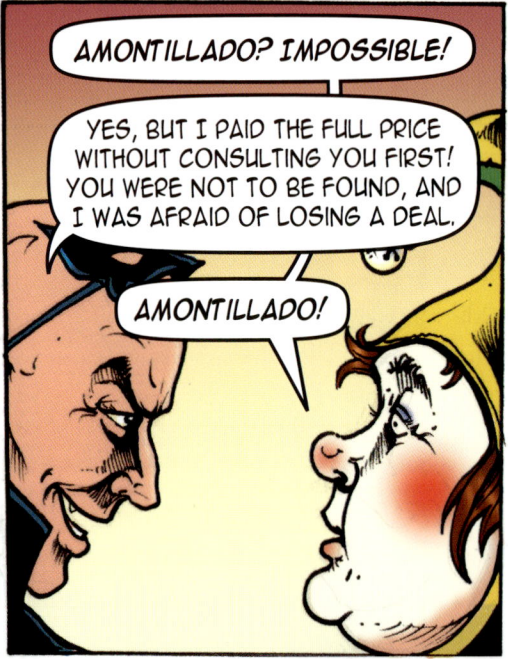

THE THOUSAND INJURIES OF FORTUNATO I HAD BORNE AS BEST I COULD, BUT WHEN HE VENTURED UPON INSULT, I VOWED **REVENGE**.

IT MUST BE UNDERSTOOD THAT NEITHER BY WORD NOR DEED HAD I GIVEN FORTUNATO CAUSE TO DOUBT MY GOOD WILL.

HE HAD A WEAK POINT... HE PRIDED HIMSELF ON HIS KNOWLEDGE OF FINE WINE.

IT WAS ABOUT DUSK DURING THE SUPREME MADNESS OF THE CARNIVAL SEASON THAT I ENCOUNTERED FORTUNATO.

HOW WELL YOU ARE LOOKING TODAY!

LISTEN; I HAVE BOUGHT A CASK OF WHAT PASSES FOR GENUINE AMONTILLADO ...BUT I HAVE MY DOUBTS.

AMONTILLADO? IMPOSSIBLE!

YES, BUT I PAID THE FULL PRICE WITHOUT CONSULTING YOU FIRST! YOU WERE NOT TO BE FOUND, AND I WAS AFRAID OF LOSING A DEAL.

AMONTILLADO!

AS I SEE YOU ARE BUSY, I AM ON MY WAY TO LUCHESI... HE WILL TELL ME—

LUCHESI CANNOT TELL AMONTILLADO FROM SHERRY! COME, LET US GO TO YOUR VAULTS!

SO I LED FORTUNATO DOWN TO THE MONTRESOR FAMILY VAULTS UNDER MY ESTATE...

IT IS FARTHER ON...

Illustrated by MIKE ROOTH

KOFF! KOFF KOFF! KOFF! KOFF KOFF KOFF! KOFF! KOFF! KOFF KOFF!
COME, WE WILL GO BACK; YOUR HEALTH IS PRECIOUS. YOU ARE RICH, RESPECTED, ADMIRED, BELOVED. WE WILL GO BACK; YOU WILL BE ILL AND I CANNOT BE RESPONSIBLE. BESIDES, THERE IS LUCHESI ...
ENOUGH! THE COUGH IS NOTHING; IT WILL NOT KILL ME!
TRUE ...
THESE VAULTS ARE EXTENSIVE!
YES, THE MONTRESORS WERE A GREAT NUMEROUS FAMILY... IT'S STILL FARTHER ON.

"PROCEED — HEREIN IS THE AMONTILLADO!"

SNAP!

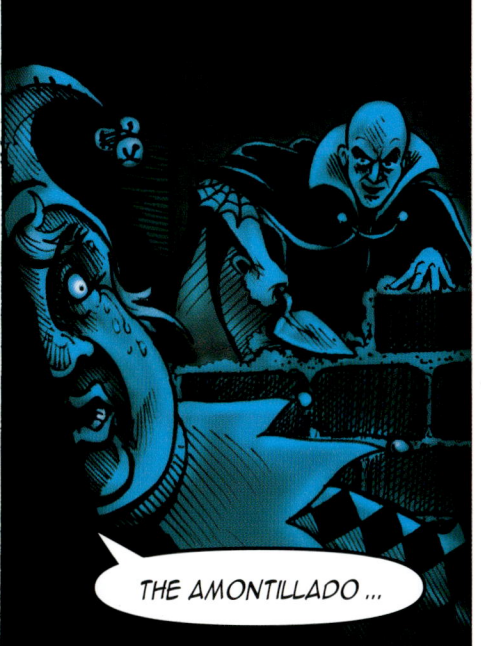

HA! HA! HA! A GOOD JOKE INDEED! WE WILL HAVE A GOOD LAUGH ABOUT IT OVER OUR WINE!

THE AMONTILLADO...

FOR THE LOVE OF ALL THINGS GOOD, MONTRESOR!

IN PACE REQUIESCAT!

wrap up

Now that you know how it ends, look back through the story and discuss with a partner how each of these elements played an important part: revenge, flattery, jealousy.

WEB CONNECTIONS

To find out more about the author, or read the entire story of "The Cask of Amontillado," go to this website: **www.poemuseum.org**.

THE POI

In January 1995, Parvesh Dhillon, 36, became violently ill at her home in Hamilton, Ontario, Canada, while preparing an after-school snack for her two young daughters. As she lay on the floor in pain, her husband, Jodha, phoned for an ambulance that rushed her to the hospital. She went into a coma and died four days later. Tests were done on her body, but the cause of her death was undetermined. After an immediate funeral service, her remains were cremated.

warm up

With any crime, police investigators always look for the motive. What is a motive? Think of reasons that would motivate people to commit crimes.

Two months later, Jodha Dhillon, 37, took his daughters to India. Shortly after their arrival, Dhillon was introduced to 21-year-old Sarabjit Brar. A marriage with a dowry was arranged, and on April 5, the couple was married in an expensive Indian ceremony.

Just 25 days later, in a remote village in India, Jodha illegally married another woman, Kushpreet Toor, 23. After promising both Sarabjit and Kushpreet he would make arrangements for them to go to Canada, Dhillon returned to Hamilton with his daughters.

SONER

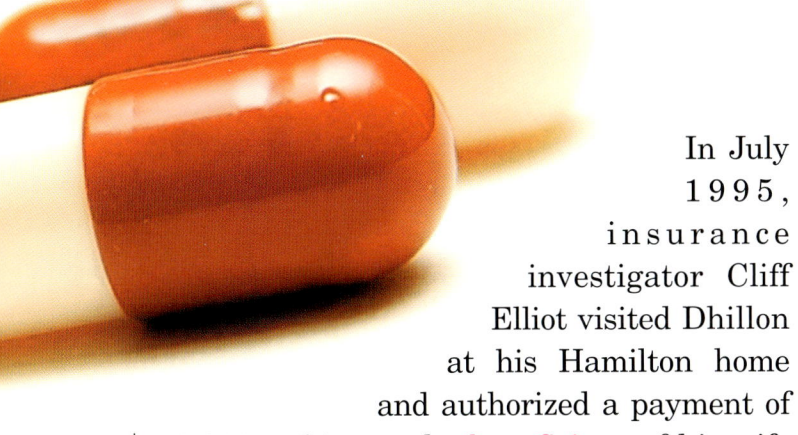

In July 1995, insurance investigator Cliff Elliot visited Dhillon at his Hamilton home and authorized a payment of $200,000 to him as the beneficiary of his wife Parvesh's life insurance policy.

In December 1995, Dhillon flew back to India. His wife, Sarabjit, was expecting twin boys. Twelve days after they were born, Dhillon visited them at the house where Sarabjit was living. Shortly after Dhillon's visit, one twin died with violent convulsions. The other twin died in the same way the next day.

In January 1996, Dhillon gave his second Indian wife, Kushpreet, a pill that he told her would prevent pregnancy. Hours later she began to shake violently. She died on the way to the hospital.

Two weeks after Kushpreet's death, Dhillon illegally married Sukhwinder Grewal, 26. He also promised her that he would take her to Canada. Then Dhillon flew back to Hamilton.

Even with the insurance money he had received, Dhillon's used car dealership was in trouble. On May 9, 1996, he and a business partner, Ranjit Khela, 25, both took out $100,000 insurance policies naming each other as beneficiary.

On June 26, Khela, after a meeting with Dhillon, collapsed in pain in his home. He died a few hours later.

When Cliff Elliot, the insurance representative, came around to Dhillon's house to investigate the Khela policy, he remembered being there before. Returning to his office, he checked his files and discovered that Jodha Dhillon had collected from another policy just one year ago! Elliot phoned the police and told Detective Warren Korol about his concerns. He was suspicious of Jodha Dhillon's involvement in both insurance policies.

Korol and his partner, Kevin Dhinsa, ordered tests on Khela's body. They discovered that he had died from strychnine poisoning.

---

beneficiary: *person who receives money or other benefits especially from a will or an insurance policy*

The detectives determined this to be a rare and lethal poison that is very difficult to obtain in Canada — but it can be purchased quite easily in India. Further investigation revealed Dhillon had recently been to India twice.

Then, Korol had the few remaining tissue samples of Jodha's deceased Canadian wife, Parvesh, analyzed by a forensic laboratory. The results showed that there was strychnine in her body.

The Hamilton detectives asked Dhillon to take a lie detector test. Although he agreed, he made up one excuse after another to avoid taking it. When Dhillon finally did take the test, he failed it.

Now, detectives Korol and Dhinsa were sure they had their man.

Both detectives flew to India and traced Dhillon's trail to the sudden deaths of his wife and children. They went to an Indian bazaar and were able to buy quantities of strychnine.

On a later visit to India, Detective Dhinsa and a Toronto forensic pathologist had the bodies of Dhillon's infant twins exhumed and examined. They found a suspicious drug in their tissues but it wasn't strychnine.

Dhillon was arrested and charged with two counts of murder for the deaths in Canada. He was tried in two separate trials for which several witnesses were flown in from India. In both trials, Jodha Dhillon was found guilty and given life sentences.

It had taken seven years to convict him of perhaps six murders. And he might have got away with it all except for the hard work of an insurance inspector and the persistence of two determined Hamilton detectives.

Upon reflection, Detective Korol says: "The greatest tragedy in this monstrous affair is that Dhillon's two innocent teenage children will be without the love and comfort of both their mother and father for the rest of their lives."

---

forensic laboratory: *a place that uses scientific methods, such as analysis of tissue samples, to investigate crimes*
forensic pathologist: *a medical doctor who investigates the physical evidence in a crime*
exhumed: *dug up*

CHECKPOINT

Why do you think the detectives would buy strychnine poison at a bazaar in India?

wrap up

1. This is written in the style of a newspaper article. Reporters include information about the five Ws in their articles: Who, What, When, Where, Why. In point form, list the information that answers the five Ws in this article.

2. Jodha Dhillon was given two life sentences. Find out what a life sentence means in the state or country where you live.

Reflections of a POLICE OFFICER

Inspector Warren Korol is second in command of 123 detectives in Hamilton, Ontario, Canada, a city of 500,000. Below he reflects on the lessons learned during the investigation and conviction of Jodha Dhillon.

I n almost every murder investigation we usually learn something new or useful. When investigating Jodha Dhillon both the police and their medical team learned to recognize the symptoms of strychnine poisoning.

Here is what happened …

When Parvesh Dhillon went into agonizing convulsions and died, the hospital physicians were confused about the cause of her death. They suspected a number of possibilities, including a heart attack. Even after the post-mortem examination, Parvesh's cause of death was listed as "lack of oxygen to the brain for unknown reasons." In other words, they didn't know why Parvesh stopped breathing.

Strychnine is extremely rare and difficult to obtain in North America. As a result, the doctors and paramedics did not recognize any of the symptoms of strychnine poisoning that Parvesh clearly had. Nor did the doctors ask the pathologist to do a specific strychnine test.

When strychnine attacks the central nervous system:
1) the victim goes into painful spasms and convulsions
2) the victim arches his/her back as a result of extreme pain
3) the victim twists his/her face into horrible grimaces
4) the victim will not let anyone touch him or her

post-mortem: *after death*
grimaces: *distorted facial expressions*

However, as soon as we were alerted to the fact that Dhillon's business partner, Ranjit Khela, also died with the same symptoms, we all began to do some serious research. We ordered a specific screening for strychnine on Ranjit Khela's body. Of course, we found strychnine to be present.

Through our research, we also learned that strychnine was very easy to buy in India. We then found out that in India, Dhillon's twin babies and one of his wives all died with the symptoms of strychnine poisoning. Of course, we couldn't charge him with those suspected murders in Canada.

Although Parvesh's murder was missed at first, in the end we solved it and put Jodha Dhillon in prison for life.

wrap up

Inspector Korol says that the police learn something new or useful in every murder investigation. Imagine you are helping Inspector Korol write his report for this case. Make two lists.

- Mistakes made early in the case.
- What we could do to avoid these mistakes.

Infamous Prisons

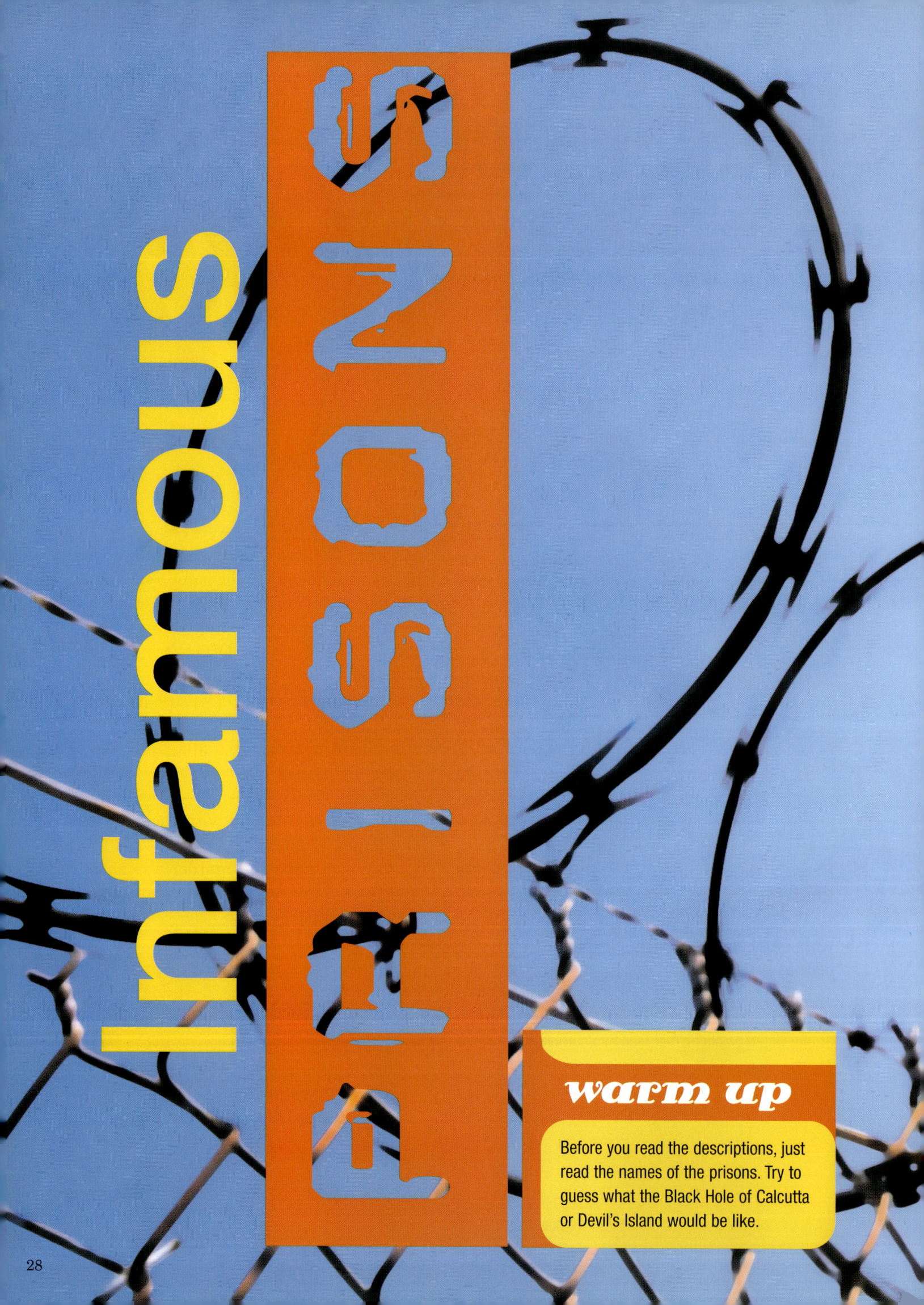

warm up

Before you read the descriptions, just read the names of the prisons. Try to guess what the Black Hole of Calcutta or Devil's Island would be like.

1. The Tower of London

William the Conqueror began building the Tower of London in 1068. Since then, it has been a castle, a fortress, a prison, a palace, and now a museum.

Many prisoners died or were executed inside the Tower grounds. Famous royal prisoners included King Henry VI and two of the wives of Henry the VIII — Anne Boleyn and Catherine Howard, both of whom were beheaded. Another prisoner was Guy Fawkes, leader of the Gunpowder Plot to blow up the British Parliament buildings in 1605.

Although the Tower has a dark and bloody history, today it is one of London's most popular tourist attractions.

2. The Clink

The Clink was a prison in London, England, that existed from 1144 to 1780. It got its name from the sound of the metal chains worn by the inmates.

For many years, it was a prison for debtors, people who could not pay their bills. Over the years, prisoners of the Clink suffered a wide range of torture that included beating, feet crushing, stretching on the rack, solitary confinement, and diets of bread and water.

The Clink was burned down in a riot in 1780, but it still exists today as a museum.

Even today people say, "… throw you in the Clink."

3. The Black Hole of Calcutta

In 1756, the Nawab (Prince) of Bengal wanted to drive the Europeans out of India. His army attacked Fort William in Calcutta (Kolkata) and captured 146 soldiers of the British East India Company.

The soldiers were crammed into a windowless 28 ft. by 20 ft. cell in the summer heat. By the next morning, 123 of the 146 soldiers had died. Many of them were still standing up due to the crowded conditions of the room.

That is the story told by a survivor. There is some question about the number of prisoners and the size of the room. But everyone agrees — that cell was "The Black Hole of Calcutta."

4. Robben Island

Robben Island (Dutch for "Seal Island") is 12 miles off the coast of Cape Town, South Africa. The Dutch were the first Europeans to settle in this part of Africa. At the end of the 17th century, the Dutch settlers used Robben Island as a prison. From 1836 to 1931, the island was used as a leper colony.

Later in the 20th century, the government of South Africa used Robben Island as a prison for political prisoners. The most famous was Nelson Mandela, who was detained for 27 years. He was released in 1990, received the Nobel Peace Prize in 1993, and became the president of South Africa in 1994.

Today, the island is a popular tourist destination and has been declared a World Heritage Site.

leper: *person who has leprosy, a contagious disease causing deformities*

5. The Bastille

For centuries the Bastille was a fort in Paris. By 1789, King Louis XVI had converted it into a prison for criminals and his political enemies.

At this time, the people wanted to get rid of the monarchy and the French Revolution was beginning. Revolutionaries stormed the Bastille on July 14. To them the prison was a symbol of the king's power. Two days later, they tore it down. France became a democracy soon after.

The prison is gone, but people still visit Place de la Bastille where it used to stand. Today, Bastille Day (July 14) is the national holiday of France.

6. Devil's Island

Devil's Island is the most famous prison in history. Actually, Devil's Island is the name for three islands located off the coast of French Guiana in South America. It was a notorious French prison colony until 1946.

From 1852 to 1946, France sent 80,000 criminals to these islands. Only 30,000 survived. Many died as a result of malaria and yellow fever. Often, the dead were rowed out to sea and fed to the sharks.

Because of the sharks, the heavy currents, and the rough seas, escape was virtually impossible. Many tried. They failed.

notorious: *well known for negative reasons*

7. The Gulag

The Gulag refers to a group of prison camps that used to exist in Russia. The prisoners were used for forced labor. The Gulag, which could hold 2.5 million prisoners at a time, stretched across the remote regions of Siberia.

From 1929 to 1953, 18 million slave laborers passed through the Gulag. During that time, they were forced to work in lumber camps; mine coal, diamonds, copper, and gold; and construct airports, canals, dams, and railroads.

Many died in the Gulag. They didn't have the right to do anything; they were underfed; they were severely mistreated by abusive guards. In the cold, harsh Russian climate, the death rate was high.

8. Auschwitz

Auschwitz was a group of concentration and death camps run by Nazi Germany during World War II (1939-1945). The camp was located in southern Poland.

Auschwitz was the largest and most efficient death camp administered by the German Third Reich. The number of victims murdered at Auschwitz, between 1940 and 1945, is estimated at 1.5 million.

Many Poles, Gypsies, and Soviet prisoners of war died at Auschwitz. However, the vast majority of the victims of Auschwitz were Jewish. The men, women, and children who were killed in the gas chambers died simply because they were Jews.

The word Auschwitz has become associated with **genocide**.

genocide: *mass murder of a specific race of people*

CHECKPOINT
"The word Auschwitz has become associated with genocide." What does this sentence mean?

FYI

In 1788, Britain began shipping criminals to Australia. The first ship arrived with 717 convicts, many of them Irish rebels or petty thieves. They were used to help the free settlers raise sheep on isolated pioneer farms. Until 1840, when the practice was abolished, 160,000 convicts were banished to this uncivilized existence which had the reputation of being a "hell on Earth." The best preserved convict ruins in Australia are now a tourist attraction located in Port Arthur, Tasmania, an island off the south coast of Australia.

wrap up

None of these infamous prisons are in use today. Do you think this is a good or bad thing? Why?

WEB CONNECTIONS

Check the Internet for examples of infamous prisons today. Write a short description of two prisons. Follow the style used in these descriptions.

I'M OUTTA HERE!

Escape from Alcatraz

June 11, 1962 — Frank Morris and brothers John and Clarence Anglin vanished from their cells and were never seen again. This event was made famous by Clint Eastwood in the movie *Escape from Alcatraz*.

The escape involved homemade drills to enlarge vent holes, false wall segments, and realistic dummy heads (complete with human hair) placed in the beds so the inmates would not be missed during nighttime counts. The three men climbed the utility pipes to the top of the cellblock, and gained access to the roof through an air vent. They climbed down a drainpipe and made their way to the water.

They used prison-issued raincoats to make lifejackets and a pontoon-type raft to help in their swim. No sign of the men was ever found.

Morris and the Anglins are officially listed as missing and presumed drowned. But who knows?

Escape from Devil's Island

Henri "Papillon" Charrière was mainly known as the author of *Papillon* — a book about his imprisonment and escape from Devil's Island.

Papillon was a small-time criminal in Paris, France. At the age of 25, he was framed for a murder and sentenced to life on Devil's Island. Papillon swore he would not serve this sentence. After 42 days, he escaped for the first time traveling a thousand miles in an open boat. Captured, he suffered two years in solitary confinement on a starvation diet.

In the last of his nine attempts, Papillon successfully escaped by throwing himself into the ocean from a cliff with a bag of coconuts to use as a raft. Having reached the mainland, he tried to hide in Venezuela. However, he was captured again. Charrière was finally set free in 1945.

In 1973 — the same year Hollywood began filming his life story with Steve McQueen playing him — Papillon died. He didn't get to see his own movie.

FYI

Special-effects experts Adam Savage and Jamie Hyneman, hosts of Discovery Channel's *MythBusters*, accurately retraced the steps of the Alcatraz escapees who had been presumed drowned. Constructing lifejackets and a pontoon-type raft from raincoats similar to those issued to Alcatraz prisoners in 1962, Savage and Hyneman determined that the escapees very likely survived.

wrap up

1. The men in these articles could all be described as criminals. With a partner decide on three other words that could be used to describe these men.

2. Both *Escape from Alcatraz* and *Papillon* were made into successful Hollywood movies. What do the stories have in common? Make a list of the reasons you think these stories made good movies.

Ma Barker

▲ Ma Barker with her friend Arthur W. Dunlop

◄ Alvin "Creepy" Karpis, kidnapper and bank robber, was a member of the Ma Barker Gang. He spent 33 years in Alcatraz. After his release, the Canadian-born Karpis was deported to Canada. He lived his last years in Spain.

▲ Gangster Arthur Barker pictured with the chief jailer in Chicago. Barker was in federal custody when his mother and brother were killed. He faced trial for the alleged kidnapping of Edward J. Bremer.

The FBI's Most Wanted Woman

Like Bonnie and Clyde, John Dillinger, and Machine Gun Kelly, Kate "Ma" Barker is a legendary American criminal of the Depression era (1930s).

There is some question about her infamous reputation. It is true that she was the mother of four vicious criminals — Herman, Lloyd, Arthur (Doc), and Fred — who murdered, robbed banks, kidnapped wealthy people for ransom, and engaged in wild, deadly shootouts with the police. But was she directly involved in the crimes of her sons' crew (the Barker-Karpis gang)? Even her sons claim she wasn't smart enough to plan, organize, or carry out any of their crimes.

Alvin "Creepy" Karpis, one of the gang's leaders, said, "Ma was just a woman who looked after her family as we moved from city to city … she just didn't have the brains to direct us on a robbery. When we were arranging a job, we'd send her to a movie. Ma saw a lot of movies."

Veteran bank robber Harvey Bailey, who sometimes ran with the Barker-Karpis gang, said, "The old woman couldn't even organize breakfast."

It was FBI director J. Edgar Hoover who made Ma Barker famous when he called her a "veritable beast of prey" and entered her name on his most-wanted list of "public enemies." Hoover claimed, "Ma Barker and her sons, and Alvin Karpis and his cronies, constitute the toughest gang of hoodlums the FBI ever has been called on to eliminate."

It may have been Hoover who started the rumor that Ma Barker taught her sons how to shoot a machine gun. That simply wasn't true.

Ma Barker was a dumpy, not-so-bright little woman who was devoted to her sons and foolishly followed them around the country looking after them as they went from crime to crime. **And that's what got her killed.**

On January 16, 1935, FBI agents surrounded a house in Ocala, Florida where Ma and her youngest son, Fred, were hiding out. A shootout between the FBI and Fred lasted for hours. Whether or not Ma took part in the gunfight is unknown. But she was found dead with a machine gun in her hand. **Some say the police put it there.** She was 55 years of age.

WEB CONNECTIONS

FBI's 10 Most Wanted Fugitives list was first released on March 14, 1950. Check out www.fbi.gov/homepage.htm and find out who is on the list right now.

warm up

Set a time limit of 5-10 minutes. In a small group, brainstorm a list of famous criminals from the past. How many are female? What is the nature of their crimes?

FYI

The FBI has been around since 1908. In that time it has changed names three times and grown from around 40 employees to almost 30,000.

CHECKPOINT

What is Bailey really saying here about Ma Barker's involvement with the crimes? Keep reading to see what the head of the FBI believes about her.

wrap up

1. If the FBI did put a machine gun in Ma Barker's hand, why would they do that?

2. One woman — two opinions. Work with a partner to create two descriptive paragraphs about Ma Barker. One of you writes a paragraph describing Ma Barker from the point of view of FBI Director, J. Edgar Hoover; the other writes a paragraph from the point of view of her son, Herman Barker.

Compare and discuss your descriptions. Which of your descriptions do you think is closer to the truth?

Lizzie Borden
Did She or Didn't She?

warm up

Most trials don't make the news. However, once in a while a trial becomes a hot media event. What factors do you think can cause that? Think of one or two trials that have become mega media events. Why were they?

CHECKPOINT

What did Lizzie and Emma call their stepmother? Why do you think the author thought this was an important fact to include?

Lizzie Borden was a quiet, well-liked Sunday school teacher. She hated her stepmother, but she loved her father. Father and stepmother ended up dead. Who could have done it?

Lizzie Borden was born in 1860 in Fall River, Massachusetts. She was the younger daughter of Andrew J. Borden, a wealthy banker who had remarried when Lizzie was four years old. Lizzie and her older sister, Emma, did not get along with their stepmother. As time went by, the two sisters never married and still lived at home with their father and stepmother. Lizzie and Emma still didn't like their stepmother. In fact, they hardly spoke to her and called her Mrs. Borden when they did.

On August 4, 1892 Emma was out, but Lizzie was home. Late in the afternoon, Lizzie and the family's maid discovered the bodies of Mr. Andrew J. Borden and Abby Borden — Lizzie's father and her stepmother. Both had been killed by multiple blows with an ax. Mrs. Borden's body was found upstairs; Mr. Borden was found on the sofa in the living room. Evidence showed that Abby Borden was killed first. The killer then waited for Mr. Borden to come home from work.

Within a week, police arrested Lizzie for the murders. Even though they didn't find the murder weapon or any other *incriminating* evidence like bloodstained clothing, they thought they had a strong case. Although Mr. Borden was a wealthy man who wouldn't even put indoor plumbing in the house, he was spending a great deal of money on his wife. How would Lizzie and Emma be able to inherit the money later? It might be all gone. They knew that Lizzie hated her stepmother and blamed her father for wasting the money.

incriminating: indicates guilt

Lizzie's trial lasted two weeks. The case attracted national attention. All the major newspapers reported on the trial. The prosecution presented evidence that Lizzie had tried to buy a poisonous chemical just one day before the murders. The druggist thought she might hurt herself with it, so he wouldn't sell it to her. The prosecution also pointed out that a neighbor had seen Lizzie burning a dress in the kitchen stove a few days after the murders. Witnesses for the defense spoke of Lizzie's fine and gentle character. These murders were obviously the work of a homicidal maniac — not Sunday school teacher Lizzie.

The jury of 12 men found Lizzie innocent. They didn't believe that a proper young woman like Lizzie could commit such a crime. Many people agreed with the jury, but not everyone. Others felt certain that she was guilty, and rumors became widespread. In fact, a children's rhyme was commonly heard shortly after the trial.

People still know it today.

Lizzie Borden took an ax,
and gave her mother forty whacks.
When she saw what she had done,
she gave her father forty-one.

The Lizzie Borden story has been made into an opera, a ballet, and several movies, and is the subject of numerous books.

homicidal maniac: *an insane person likely to commit murder*

CHECKPOINT
Think about it! What was it about this trial that attracted so much attention from the newspapers?

CHECKPOINT
Did you notice? There were no women on the jury. Why did the author point that out? How could this affect the verdict?

wrap up

1. What would newspapers report? Lizzie Borden has been acquitted. Each person in the class writes headlines — one showing she was innocent all along; the other from a reporter who thinks she was guilty.

2. Share your headlines with the class. Make two collages — one guilty, one innocent.

WEB CONNECTIONS
To find out more, just type **"Lizzie Borden"** in your search engine. You'll find lots of material. Some say she was innocent. Some say she was guilty. You'll have to make up your own mind.

FYI
The children's rhyme is incorrect, but it worked as a poem. Abby Borden suffered 19 ax wounds; Andrew Borden suffered 11.

Double Take

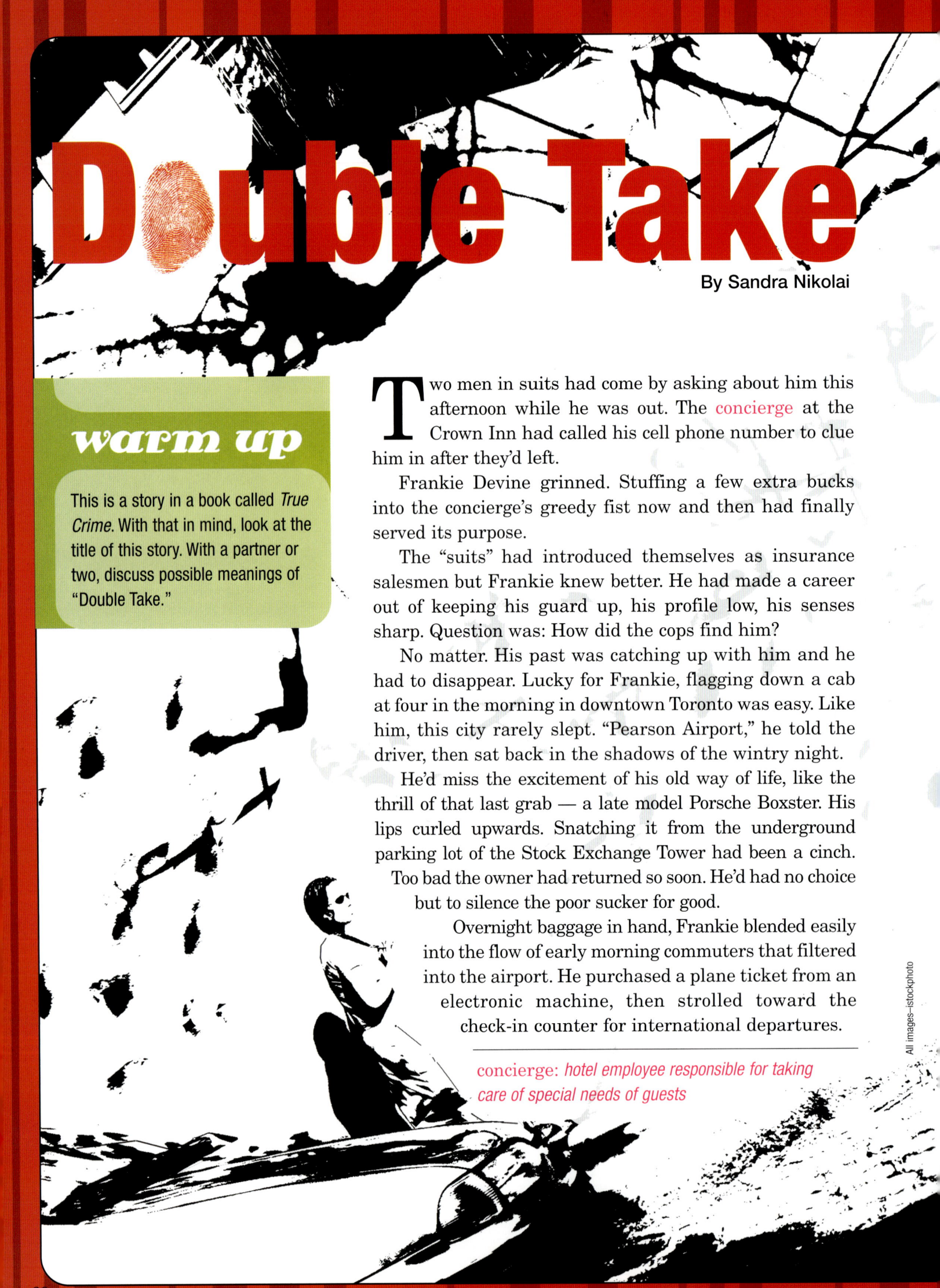

By Sandra Nikolai

warm up

This is a story in a book called *True Crime*. With that in mind, look at the title of this story. With a partner or two, discuss possible meanings of "Double Take."

Two men in suits had come by asking about him this afternoon while he was out. The concierge at the Crown Inn had called his cell phone number to clue him in after they'd left.

Frankie Devine grinned. Stuffing a few extra bucks into the concierge's greedy fist now and then had finally served its purpose.

The "suits" had introduced themselves as insurance salesmen but Frankie knew better. He had made a career out of keeping his guard up, his profile low, his senses sharp. Question was: How did the cops find him?

No matter. His past was catching up with him and he had to disappear. Lucky for Frankie, flagging down a cab at four in the morning in downtown Toronto was easy. Like him, this city rarely slept. "Pearson Airport," he told the driver, then sat back in the shadows of the wintry night.

He'd miss the excitement of his old way of life, like the thrill of that last grab — a late model Porsche Boxster. His lips curled upwards. Snatching it from the underground parking lot of the Stock Exchange Tower had been a cinch. Too bad the owner had returned so soon. He'd had no choice but to silence the poor sucker for good.

Overnight baggage in hand, Frankie blended easily into the flow of early morning commuters that filtered into the airport. He purchased a plane ticket from an electronic machine, then strolled toward the check-in counter for international departures.

---

concierge: *hotel employee responsible for taking care of special needs of guests*

On his way, he passed an open-air coffee shop and glanced at the overhead television inside. The last thing he expected to see was his face on the local news and a banner at the bottom of the screen that read, "Police search for murder suspect." He yanked out a pair of black-framed eyeglasses, slipped them on, then fell into place with the other travelers. All the while, he kept a discreet eye on the security guards patrolling the premises, knowing it was just a matter of time before the police would extend their search to the airport.

At the check-in counter, a weary attendant flipped through Frankie's passport and asked the usual questions regarding "business" trips.

Frankie stayed cool, kept his answers brief. Ten minutes later, he was boarding his flight.

As the plane lifted off, he fantasized about his luxurious new lifestyle in Puerto Plata.

Equipped with a maid and cook, the upscale villa on the Amber Coast boasted a private outdoor pool, air conditioning throughout the spacious rooms, and a panoramic view of the ocean.

And it was all courtesy of Mario, his boss in New York. Even so, it would have been enough for Mario to devise a great getaway plan for Frankie, but when he offered to set him up with the finest cosmetic surgeon that money could buy, pick out a tropical villa, and establish a foolproof alias for him — well, how could Frankie refuse?

Yeah, Mario had been one hell of a good sport — considering how Frankie had dumped his ugly sister after only two dates last summer. Who could blame him? A single woman in her thirties, she had suffered the ravages of old age years before her time. The hooked nose and lazy eye didn't help either. A Picasso reject, Frankie thought when he had first seen her but was careful not to voice his opinion in front of Mario.

And with good reason. Anyone who had ever worked for Mario knew that he regarded the slightest insult against

CHECKPOINT
- At this point in the story, how does Frankie feel about Mario?
- What do you think Frankie means by "foolproof alias"?

---

discreet: *careful not to draw attention to himself*
panoramic: *wide, unbroken view*
Picasso: *a Spanish artist whose paintings show very distorted features of people*

his sister as a personal affront. He showed no mercy to offenders and banished them beyond his protective circle of influence.

Worried that he might suffer dire repercussions for brushing off Mario's sister, Frankie had called him the next day to explain. "Sorry, Mario. I think your sister would make a great wife but I'm just not the marrying type," he had confided, man-to-man.

"Hey, don't sweat it. I'll match her up with someone else," Mario had replied, much to Frankie's relief.

But that was all in the past.

Yet, despite his recent good fortune, Frankie's appointment with the cosmetic surgeon in Puerto Plata hung like a millstone around his neck. Sure, he had endured more terrifying ordeals in the back streets of major cities, but it was one thing to fend off tangible threats, quite another to be put under and left in the hands of a plastic surgeon. Come to think of it, he didn't even know who his surgeon was. "No exchange of names," Mario had warned Frankie. "It's for your own protection."

The sun reflected off the pale shores of Puerto Plata as Frankie rode in a cab from La Union airport straight to the private clinic as Mario had instructed him. But far from enjoying the view, he couldn't think of anything but the ordeal that awaited him. No matter, he consoled himself, the sooner the surgery would be over, the sooner he'd have a new identity. Then he wouldn't have to worry about his past catching up with him.

As the cab approached the white two-story building at 4 Via Condor, Frankie caught sight of a pretty young nurse standing at the entrance. She smiled, as if she had been expecting him, and escorted him inside.

But when he asked her about the surgeon, she replied in a heavy Spanish accent, "No speak English." She ushered him past the receptionist's desk, down a short corridor, and into the doctor's office, then left and shut the door behind her.

---

affront: *insult*
dire repercussions: *dreadful effects*
millstone: *circular stone used to grind grain*
tangible: *real*

Second thoughts plagued Frankie as he sat waiting. Although he trusted Mario like a brother, he couldn't shrug off the edginess creeping under his skin — let alone the pungent medicinal scent.

He diverted his attention to the office décor: a wooden writing desk and matching armchair, a four-tier wicker bookcase stacked with textbooks along the wall to the left, a heavy-duty paper shredder in the corner.

His stomach churned. He had just about made the decision to leave when a portly man in a white lab coat entered the office.

"Good day. I'm the doctor who will be performing your cosmetic surgery." The fifty-something man extended a hand.

Frankie noticed his heavy accent, felt his beefy grip.

The doctor sat down and opened the folder on his desk. "Our mutual associate, Mario, has informed me that you will be taking on the identity of Carlos Molina." He held up a picture of a handsome, dark-haired man for him to see.

Frankie nodded, thankful for his boss's discerning taste. Although he was curious, he refrained from inquiring about Carlos. He knew better than to cast doubt on his boss's judgment in such matters. "So how do you know Mario?" he asked instead.

"My nephew did some work for him in New York, dated his sister once." The doctor shook his head, broke into a wide smile. "He told me she was the ugliest woman he had ever seen. Good thing Mario does not hold grudges," he chuckled.

Frankie grinned but didn't say anything. That was all in the past.

"Your new passport and personal documents will be ready the day you are discharged from here," the doctor continued. "Do you have any questions about the surgery?"

In spite of his apprehension, Frankie put up a brave front.

"What are the risks?"

"My team has performed similar surgeries many times before. You have nothing to worry about," the doctor said with confidence. He studied Frankie. "Your olive skin tone, dark eyes, and medium build will make the transition to Carlos Molina even more successful." He glanced at Frankie's

---

pungent: *a sharp or strong smell*
portly: *fat*
discerning: *having good taste*

> **CHECKPOINT**
> - What does this sentence mean?
> - What second thoughts might Frankie be having at this point?

hands. "We will also change your fingerprints to those of your new alias. Of course, you must destroy your current passport and personal ID." He pointed to the shredder.

Frankie dug out his passport and plastic cards, and slipped them into the shredder.

Weeks later, he was lounging by his villa poolside, a wide-brimmed straw hat on his head, a cool drink in one hand and a mirror in the other. The skin around his fingertips was healing well. The swelling around his eyes hadn't completely subsided yet, but he already liked what he saw. Why, he even looked better than the original Carlos, he thought.

Soon Frankie began to throw lavish dinner parties to introduce himself as Carlos Molina to the elite society of Puerto Plata. His invented background — marketing consultant — served him well, given his earlier success in capturing intended "target markets." Now that he could relax and enjoy life without qualms about his past, his personality lightened up too. His newfound charm earned him invitations throughout the neighborhood.

On two such occasions, he drew the attention of a retired Spanish detective who, with his wife, had chosen a nearby villa for their retirement abode.

"It's strange, but you still look familiar to me, Carlos," Pedro declared at their third encounter at a neighbor's pool party. "You're certain you've never lived in Spain?"

"Same answer as the last time, Pedro. I was born and raised in America," Frankie smiled, though Pedro's insistent probing had begun to get on his nerves.

As before, Pedro shrugged and moved on to another topic.

But this time, Frankie's instincts raised an alarm. He decided to visit the surgeon to find out more about Carlos Molina.

The next morning, the cab driver drove down Via Condor but couldn't find the clinic. Frankie had him circle the block three times as he scanned both sides of the street for number 4, but the two-story building was no longer there — only an empty lot.

Frankie panicked. He put in a call to Mario in New York but the receptionist said he was away on business and couldn't be reached.

Later that day, a knock at Frankie's door announced the arrival of two burly men in lightweight suits.

"Senor Carlos Molina?" The one with a scar under his right eye flashed his police badge.

---

qualms: *uneasy doubts*
abode: *home*

"Yes?"

"I am Detective Garcia and this is my partner, Detective Alonso. We would like to speak with you. May we come in?"

"Of course." Frankie led them into the guest room. "What's this about?"

Detective Alonso's eyes squinted from under bushy eyebrows. "An international warrant has been issued for your arrest."

"On what grounds?" Frankie remained calm, confident that his past could no longer harm him.

"For the murder of Maria Fuentes in Spain."

"But I didn't kill her — I don't even know her!"

Frankie retorted, the impact of his predicament came hitting home. "You see — I'm not really Carlos Molina. I had cosmetic surgery so I could look like Carlos Molina, but my real name is — I'm —"

• • • • • • • • •

"Hello, Mario?"

"Yes, doctor."

"It is done. The police took him away moments ago."

"Have you booked the flight for your nephew?"

"Yes. Carlos will be leaving Spain today by private jet. Thank you again for helping him to escape to Toronto and for arranging his cosmetic surgery there."

"By the way, what will his new name be?"

There was a slight pause.

"Frankie Devine."

---

predicament: *unpleasant situation*

CHECKPOINT
Note words and phrases that describe how Frankie is feeling at this moment.

wrap up

1. Now that you have read the story, what do you think of the title? If Mario were going to give this story a title, what might he call it? If Frankie were going to give it a title, what might he call it?

2. Imagine you are Mario at the beginning of the story. Write an email to your nephew Carlos explaining the plan you have in mind.

3. Now you know what Mario's plan was all along. Look back through the story. Find and list clues that suggest things were different from what Frankie thought.

Interview with a Profiler

The Woman Who STALKS THE STALKERS

By Angella Johnson
MAIL & GUARDIAN, October 1, 1997

warm up

A profiler figures out, from evidence, the type of person likely to have committed the crime. Make a list of three questions that you would ask a profiler during an interview. As you read the article, see if your questions are answered.

CHECKPOINT

Think about it. The interviewer says people who are easily upset shouldn't be a profiler. Which words in this paragraph say that?

"I never allow my picture to be taken for newspapers or magazines; it's too dangerous," insists Dr. Miki Pistorius, chief investigative psychologist for the South African Police Service.

I can see her point. If your job is to track down serial killers by tapping into the minds of the country's most dangerous criminals, it is not a good idea to let them know what you look like.

So what exactly does this modern-age crime fighter do? "I assess a crime scene and try to reconstruct in my mind what happened and why. Then I put together a profile of the killer, his background, age, color, etc." Some people call her a forensic psychologist. "But that sounds as if I examine dead bodies, so I prefer the term investigative psychologist," she says.

It is a 24-hour job and she gets called whenever or wherever police come across a serial killing, serial rapist, or serious child abuse. It is not a job for the squeamish, and I wonder how Pistorius copes with the pressures.

Maybe the pressure is beginning to tell. Images of bloody crime scenes and of greedy maggots feasting on decomposing bodies invade her sleep. "It's nothing to worry about," she assesses calmly. "Just a message for me to slow down and take things easy for a while."

It is just as well that she has recruited and trained another female psychologist to help with the wave of serial murders and other crimes that have plagued the country since the term "serial killer" was first recognized by the SAPS in 1994. That was when Pistorius joined the service, straight from completing her Masters in Psychology at Pretoria University. Until recently, she was the only person to whom the country's police could turn to for help whenever a serial killer was suspected.

So are women better at this job? "It's nothing to do with gender; there's a lot of intuition in it, but anyone can do what I do. I've trained over 100 detectives, mostly men, to be able to investigate such cases."

"The main thing is to try to focus on the person's fantasies. You have to try to picture that, no matter how grotesque it is; to relive the smallest detail." To her, the crime scene is like a painting. "You have to decipher it as you would a work of art. You know, things like the position of the body; weaponry; was torture involved; the kinds of wounds; is there evidence of a pattern?"

It is the little touches or rituals that make a difference. "You have to reconstruct chronologically what he did (it is usually a male perpetrator) and figure out why he did it. If you want to kill someone you only have to shoot him or her. Anything extra will give you characteristics of your killer."

Pistorius believes that a serial killer starts off with a fixation early in his psychological development. Six to twelve years of age is when a future killer starts to have abnormal fantasies. He's a loner and fails to develop a conscience. Pistorius argues that these boys usually lack a male role model. By the time he reaches puberty the fixation has taken hold. "He tends to be a loner and daydreamer who fails to respond to social norms."

When he becomes an adult, the trigger that will send this fixated individual into the killing field could be anything that threatens his self-image and makes him feel useless.

"Teachers, neighbors and family members should be on the lookout for signs of fixation, such as breaking off dolls' heads, especially in children who have either been neglected or abused," she argues. Does this mean serial killers are socially created?

"No! It's in the individual. Social factors contribute — you won't get a serial killer from a happy family — but it is how the person reacts to circumstances."

Her most gruesome case occurred when police discovered nine victims of a serial killer in the Boksburg veld. "They were in various stages of decomposition. It tells me that the women knew they were going to be killed. They must have seen the other bodies lying there."

What a job!

CHECKPOINT

As you read the next two paragraphs, think about how a profiler would use intuition on the job.

CHECKPOINT

Which social norms do you think she means? (Even future serial killers probably use a spoon to eat soup.)

wrap up

Imagine you are the local Chief of Police who needs to hire a profiler. Using information from the interview, write a newspaper ad for the right person. You could use headings like: Job Description, Responsibilities, Educational Requirements, Special Qualities.

SAPS: *South African Police Service*
decipher: *make sense of*
rituals: *repeated procedures; ceremonies*
fixation: *obsession; fascination*
veld: *grassland in Southern Africa*

The Real Deal

Renowned author Kathy Reichs is a real-life *forensic anthropologist* at the Office of the Chief Medical Examiner in North Carolina and the *Laboratoire des Sciences Judiciaires et de Médecine Légale* in Quebec. Reichs is frequently called upon to testify as an expert witness in criminal trials. She has conducted forensic examinations worldwide, in places such as Rwanda, Guatemala, Southeast Asia, and Ground Zero in New York, and has identified the remains of individuals killed during World War II.

Her work has helped her develop a number of best-selling novels. Each of her novels is loosely based on the cases and technology she has encountered in her work.

CSI: CRIME SCENE INVESTIGATION
TRUE TO LIFE?

CSI: Crime Scene Investigation is a television series about the Las Vegas Crime Scene Investigation Unit. The Unit is made up of five crime scene specialists, a *forensic entomologist*, a blood splatter analyst, a materials and element analyst, an audio/visual analyst, and a hair and fiber analyst. In each episode the investigators struggle to solve mysterious and often horrifying crimes with the aid of forensic science, crime scene investigation tools, and modern technology.

Due to the worldwide popularity of *CSI: Crime Scene Investigation,* two spin-off series have been developed: *CSI: Miami* and *CSI: New York*.

To accurately portray the procedures and forensic science used in real life investigations, the script writer, Anthony Zuiker, rode with the Las Vegas Metropolitan Police Department's crime scene investigators for several weeks. Also, in their quest for accuracy, several of the show's producers conducted their own in-depth research on forensic science and factual accounts of murders. Unfortunately, inaccuracies, such as those presented below, still exist in the show.

CSI SHOW	REAL LIFE
• Crime scene investigators frequently question suspects.	• Crime scene investigators ask witnesses and victims questions but they never question a suspect.
• Crime scene investigators solve the crime without the involvement of police officers.	• Police officers question a suspect after the suspect has been made aware of his/her rights.
• Using the technology in their lab, crime scene investigators analyze the evidence in a matter of hours.	• Crime scene investigators work closely with police officers to solve crime. It often takes weeks in the lab to analyze evidence collected at a crime scene.

forensic anthropologist: *an expert who examines skeletons to determine identification and time of death*
forensic entomologist: *a scientist who studies insects at a crime scene to determine facts such as time of death*

A scene from *CSI Miami*. In this episode Horatio and his team must uncover the evidence in the brutal murder of an entire family in their own home. The only survivors are a blood-soaked toddler, and the father who's in surgery. The immediate assumption is that the mother is responsible, but the evidence discloses a different outcome.

ACKNOWLEDGMENTS

The publisher gratefully acknowledges permission to reprint copyright material in this book.

Every reasonable effort has been made to trace the owners of copyrighted material and to make due acknowledgment. Any errors or omissions drawn to our attention will be gladly rectified in future editions.

Angella Johnson: "The woman who stalks the stalkers" first published by *Mail & Guardian*, October 1, 1997, reprinted by permission of the publisher.

Sandra Nikolai: "Double Take", reprinted by permission of the author.